The Nine Habits
of
Highly Effective
Christians

The Nine Habits

of

Highly Effective Christians

Victor M. Parachin

Resurrection Press

An Imprint of

CATHOLIC BOOK PUBLISHING CORP.

Totowa • New Jersey

First published in April, 2009 by

        Catholic Book Publishing/Resurrection Press
        77 West End Road
        Totowa, NJ 07512

ISBN 978-1-933066-11-0

Library of Congress Catalog Number: 2008943458

Printed in the United States of America

1 2 3 4 5 6 7 8 9

www.catholicbookpublishing.com

Contents

INTRODUCTION

We are what we repeatedly do.
Excellence then, is not an act,
but a habit.   —Aristotle

TWO cars were at an intersection when the light turned green. The man in the first vehicle didn't notice that the light had changed so the woman in the car behind him began pounding on her steering wheel, screaming at the man to "get moving" and directed obscene hand gestures toward him. Still, the man didn't move. Finally, he looked up, saw an orange light and accelerated through the intersection just as the light turned to red. The woman behind him was furious and began screaming in frustration because she missed her turn to get through the intersection. While she was venting, she saw someone approach her vehicle. It was a police officer with his hand on his gun. The officer instructed the woman to turn off her car and keep both hands in sight. She complied. The police officer ordered her to exit car with hands raised.

When she got out, he instructed her to turn around and place her hands behind her. Then he handcuffed the woman and frisked her. He took her to the police station where she was fingerprinted, photographed, searched, booked, and placed in a cell. After an hour, another officer approached the cell, opened the door, and escorted her back to the booking desk. There, the arresting officer was waiting with her personal belongings telling her she was free to leave. He offered this explanation: "I pulled up behind your car while you were blowing your horn, making obscene hand gestures, swearing and shouting at the man in front of you. I noticed the 'Choose Life' license plate holder; the 'What would Jesus do?' bumper sticker; the 'Follow me to Sunday School' bumper sticker; and the chrome-plated Christian fish emblem on the trunk. Naturally, I assumed you had stolen the car."

Though that story may be an urban legend, it does point out that some Christians—perhaps even many Christians—do not live out their faith. Their creeds don't match their deeds and their belief does not shape their behavior. Anticipating that this could happen, the Apostle Paul wrote to the earliest Christians encouraging them to fully embrace nine spiritual practices. Calling them the "fruit of the spirit" Paul identified these as the habits of highly effective Christians: *The fruit of the Spirit is love, joy, peace, patience, kindness, goodness, faithfulness, gentleness, and self-control* (Gal 15:22-23).

Although this book can be read in one sitting from beginning to end, the intent is that the reader will view this as a devotional book. That means reading one habit and then pausing for a few days, allowing the message of the Apostle Paul to enter and grow in the soul. After reading my reflections on the habits cited by Paul, it is my hope readers will apply the habit they have just read and reflected upon using the Seven Further Considerations at the end of each chapter as a starting point.

What this weary world needs now are women and men who will live out these vital spiritual disciplines. In so doing, they will indeed make the planet a kinder, gentler place.

—*Victor M. Parachin*

HABIT #1 - LOVE

The Fruit of the Spirit Is Love

They are the true disciples of Christ,
not who know most, but who love most.
—Frederich Spanheim The Elder

ONE day in Pittsburgh, Pennsylvania a car was stolen. As the thieves began stripping the vehicle they came across papers identifying the owner as Fred Rogers. Immediately, they knew the car belonged to the man who was a television host to millions of children via his program "Mr. Rogers Neighborhood." Quickly, they reassembled the car, cleaned, vacuumed, and returned it leaving this handwritten note of apology under the wiper: "We're sorry. We didn't know it was *your* car."

Except for Mr. Rogers, who else in our modern times could have such an effect on a group of thieves? What was it about Fred Rogers that could make criminals reconsider their actions? What did those thieves see in Mr. Rogers that made them want to be better people? The answer is this: Fred Rogers was a man of immense love for humanity, especially children. His life eloquently reflects the clear, consistent, command of the bible to be people of love. Jesus said: "Love one another as I have loved you" (Jn 13:34). St. Paul prayed: "May the Lord make your love increase and overflow for one another and for everyone else" (1 Thes 3:12). St. Peter wrote: "Love one another deeply, from the heart." Scripture states: "All that matters is faith expressing itself through love" (Gal 5:6). Love is some-

9

thing anyone can express and everyone can experience. The Apostle Paul lists love as the first spiritual fruit: "The fruit of the Spirit is *love*" (Gal 5:22). Here are some ways to maximize your power of love.

- *Don't be yourself; be someone a little nicer.* That's the intent of Jesus' teaching in the Sermon on the Mount when he said: "If someone forces you to go one mile, go with him two miles." That teaching is the source of the phrase "going the extra mile." If you truly wish to maximize your power of love, go the extra mile. Don't just be yourself. Be someone a little nicer. Alma Barkman, a resident of Winnipeg, Manitoba had the pleasure of being on the receiving end of someone who went the extra mile. She says: "As I tumbled wet laundry into the automatic dryer, my thoughts went back to a windy spring day more than forty years ago." At the time she was "awkwardly" pregnant with their second son. It was laundry day and before the era of automatic dryers so she was dragging a heavy wicker basket full of wet clothes outside to hang on the wash line. The squeaking of the clothesline pulley attracted the attention of a telephone repairman high up on a pole in another yard. The two exchanged a neighborly wave.

After she hung out the wash to dry, she went inside to make lunch for her toddler son. Inside she could hear the clothing snapping in the wind on the line outside. Suddenly there was an ominous silence. Looking out, she was dismayed to see the clothesline had broken and most of her snowy white wash had fallen onto the garden plot. Already exhausted, she pulled on rubber boots, picked up the clothesbasket and trudged back outside. Coming around the corner she was startled to meet the telephone repairman, face to face. "I saw the whole thing happen," he explained, "So I came down the pole to give you a hand. Free service and lifetime guarantee!" he smiled pulling a pair of pliers from his leather tool belt. With a few skillful twists, he quickly mended the broken clothesline. "Forty years later I think about that kindly repairman so unselfishly giving of himself to help a stranger in her plight."

• *Nurture a child's capacity to love.* Many parents and other adults seem to reserve their highest praise to a child for their intellectual or athletic accomplishments. These children are most complimented when they achieve distinction in one of these two areas. "David, I'm so proud of how smart you are! This is a great report card." or "Kelley, you're an incredible athlete. What a basketball player you are." Commenting on this issue, Rabbi Joseph Telushkin says: "Is it healthy for children who are very smart or athletic to be raised to believe that these talents and abilities are truly what is most important about them?" So, Rabbi Telushkin offers this advice to parents and other adults such as coaches, youth workers, Sunday School teachers: "Here is a simple suggestion, one that has the capacity to make both your children and the world happier and kinder: *Reserve your highest praise to your children for when they perform kind deeds.*" The ideal time to compliment a young person is whenever he or she acts in kind, compassionate, loving ways. That way you extend and expand loving attitudes through another generation. "Think about that for a moment," says Rabbi Telushkin: "a generation of people who most like themselves when they are doing good. What a world that would be!"

- *Help another person flourish when they flounder.* When you see someone floundering, reach out with love to help that individual flourish. Every time we stretch ourselves on behalf of another, it is a form of love in action. Often the difference between a person floundering and flourishing is the action of one person. Consider the difference one person made on the life of Henry David Thoreau. On July 4, 1845 Henry David Thoreau moved into his isolated cabin on Walden Pond, near Concord, Massachusetts. He was 27 and wanted to experiment with living simply. His inspiration came from a memorable trip he took with his beloved brother, John. During the summer of 1839 he and John built a boat, sailed it down the Concord River, and took a two-week walking tour around Mt. Washington. That trip and time with his brother became a highlight in Thoreau's life and took on greater meaning when John cut himself shaving in the winter of 1841, caught lockjaw, and died in Thoreau's arms.

Thoreau was devastated. For weeks after his brother's death, Thoreau was unable to write, talk to family or friends, and even experienced symptoms of lockjaw himself. It was a family friend, Ralph Waldo Emerson, who reached out suggesting Thoreau take his mind off his grief by writing reviews of natural history books. Thoreau responded positively and received great comfort from the task of writing: "Books of natural history make the most cheerful winter reading. To him who contemplates a trait of natural beauty no harm nor disappointment can come." The essay Thoreau wrote about the natural history books was published and became one of Thoreau's early literary successes. He continued writing essays for several years always recalling the summer he spent with his brother and the renewal he experienced living in the wilderness. Thoreau wanted to re-create the experience but on a deeper level so he began looking for a place where he could build a small cabin in the woods. Again, his friend, Ralph Waldo Emerson responded by generously giving him a few acres of land on Walden Pond, a place Thoreau had been visiting most of his life. There, Thoreau built a tiny cabin—ten feet wide and fifteen feet long—living alone at Walden for two years, two months, and two days.

Based on that experience he published his book Walden, a reflection upon simple living in natural surroundings. Though it only sold 256 copies in its first year, the book has never gone out of print and has been translated into hundreds of languages.

• *Practice forgiveness.* The humorous but sad story is told of a very sick man who finally sought out doctors. After examining him and running some tests, the physicians said: "I'm sorry, sir, you have rabies and because you waited so long, there's nothing that can be done for you. You will die in a few days." The man was stunned so the doctor withdrew himself giving the man time to compose himself. When the doctor returned, the man was writing furiously on a sheet of paper. "Are you making a will?" the doctor asked. "No!" said the man, "I'm making a list of all the people I'm going to bite!"

Resentment, revenge, rage, may feel good initially but in the long run holding a grudge simply freezes us in place, destroys peace of mind, and erodes our capacity for loving kindness. Extend forgiveness and you will maximize your love while experiencing the richness of life.

• *Understand and appreciate your power of love.* Love is such a compelling force that minister and author Emmet Fox noted: "There is no difficulty that enough love will not conquer; no disease that enough love will not heal; no door that enough love will not open; no gulf that enough love will not bridge; no wall that enough love will not throw down; no sin that enough love will not redeem . . . It makes no difference how deeply seated may be the trouble; how hopeless the outlook; how muddled the tangle; how great the mistake. A sufficient realization of love will dissolve it all. If only you could love enough you would be the happiest and most powerful being in the world."

Understand and appreciate your power of love. Tap into it. Speak and act in loving ways toward everyone you encounter. More than anything else, all people want love and acceptance. You have it in your power to give them what they want.

Seven Further Considerations

1. What are some ways you could live out your life so that your loving influence over those closest to you would be felt in positive and powerful ways?

2. How could you be, not just yourself, but someone a little nicer? What changes would you have to make to your behavior?

3. Look carefully at your thoughts, words, and deeds. Which ones need correcting in order to be a more loving person?

4. There are people you know who are hurting and have been wounded by life. How can you help them to flourish rather than flounder?

5. Who do you need to forgive? What steps can you take to make it happen?

6. Think about this quote from theologian Paul Tillich: "The first duty of love is to listen." Why did he say that? How can you put it into practice?

7. What would happen if you made it your spiritual intention to offer love toward every person you encounter each day?

HABIT #2 - JOY

The Fruit of the Spirit Is . . . Joy

*Joy is the most infallible sign
of the presence of God.*
—Leon Henri Marie Bloy

WHILE running errands one day, Kimberly Kirberger passed two teenagers by the side of the road holding a car wash sign. Because her car was dirty, she pulled over. While waiting in line for her car to be washed, Kirberger was curious what motivated nearly fifty teenagers to devote an entire Saturday to washing cars. After her car was washed, she handed the teens a twenty-dollar bill and asked what they were raising money for. They explained that a friend of theirs, C. T. Schmitz, had recently died of cancer. He was fifteen years old, six-feet-two, had a lot of friends, all of whom described him as a "boy sweeter than any they had known." One of his closest friends, a youth named Kevin, decided to put the car wash together because he wished to honor his friend and also to bring together his classmates with his Boy Scout troop. Kirberger learned the teens wanted to plant a tree in front of their school and, if they raised sufficient funds, they would put a plaque there as well. Both would be in memory of their friend C. T. With that explanation, Kirberger was handed a bag of homemade cookies. The tag tied to the bag read: "Thanks for helping us plant a tree for C. T."

Those teenagers provide a glowing example of this reality: it is possible to reclaim joy even when living has been severely tested. Those teens had lost, to death, a beloved friend and yet, they had the maturity and wisdom to find a way of turning sadness into gladness, hurting into healing, and pain into peace. The young people took something heartbreaking and began the process of transforming it into something hopeful even joyful. The art of living is not merely bearing up under trials and troubles but finding ways of cultivating joy in daily life. That may be one reason why the Apostle Paul includes joy in his list of spiritual fruit: "The fruit of the spirit is love, *joy* . . ." (Gal 5:22). In her book, *Finding Joy*, Charlotte Davis Kasl, Ph.D., says: "Joy is good for you. Joy has the power to open our hearts, remove fear, instill hope and foster healing . . . joy stimulates our immune system, increases our energy, and gives us mental clarity." Here are some ways to bring more joy into daily life.

• *Begin by understanding that the will of God for us includes joy.* "If you have no joy in your religion, there's a leak in your Christianity somewhere," declared evangelist Billy Sunday. His observation is backed up by the Bible, which consistently reminds us that the will of God for us includes a heavy dose of joy. Here are some examples: "Weeping may last for the night, but joy comes with the morning" (Ps 30:6). "Those who go out weeping . . . shall come home with shouts of joy" (Ps 126:6). Likewise, Jesus promised: "Your grief will turn into joy" (Jn 16:20). Those biblical passages mean we are not doomed to a lifetime of duty, responsibility, struggle, suffering, and unhappiness. Rather, we are destined for joy.

• *Bring enthusiasm into all of life's activities.* Whether you are a volunteer coach, serving as a church committee chair, or working long hours as a busy professional, bring enthusiasm into all of your life's activities. Here is solid advice from Rev. Norman Vincent Peale: "Think excitement, talk excitement, act out excitement, and you are bound to become an excited person. Life will take on a new zest, deeper interest, and greater meaning. You can think, talk, and act yourself into dullness, or into monotony, or into unhappiness. By the same process you can build up inspiration, excitement, and a surging depth of joy." Similarly, basketball coach, Phil Jackson says: "Winning is important to me, but what brings me real joy is the experience of being fully engaged in whatever I'm doing."

Consider the example of Donald A. Dreyer, M.D., Ph.D. Refusing to let age keep him from plunging enthusiastically into all aspects of his life, he applied and was accepted into medical school at the age of 55. After graduating he practiced medicine for twenty years and then became convinced that it wasn't too late for him to begin working out. Thus, at age 75 he began lifting weights and increasingly became stronger and stronger. So much so that he entered the National Senior Games where he won the gold medal in the javelin throw. Now 80 years of age, Dr. Dryer holds medals in five events. Dr. Dryer says that getting older provides him with unusual advantages: "Now that I'm 80, I no longer have to compete with those young 75-year-old punks!"

- *Be kind to animals.* Another way of cultivating more joy in life is by being kind to animals. They too are made and loved by God. "A righteous man cares for the needs of his animal," notes the Bible (Prov 12:10). The thirteenth century mystic Metchild of Magdeburg said: "The truly wise person kneels at the feet of all creatures." And, the Jewish Kabbalah advises: "God nourishes everything, from the horned buffalo to nits, disdaining no creature . . . So should you be good to all creatures, disdaining none." Being kind to animals delivers its own, unique joy.

Consider one woman's experience who was traveling on an eight-lane highway through Portland, Oregon. There was a great deal of traffic with most people in a hurry. She noticed a mother duck, limping, with five baby ducks following her right onto the interstate. They were making their way to a park on the other side. The woman was in the far lane and could do nothing to help but did get off at the next exit to turn back. She fully expected to see the ducks dead or injured. "To my amazement, all traffic on both sides of the highway had stopped. Many people were out of their cars making a safe path for the mother duck and her babies to cross. No one was honking or swearing." The woman sat in her car and cried tears of joy over the beautiful sight of humans protecting a mother duck and her five babies. "We read about cruelty every day and these total strangers worked together for the sake of those little ducks."

- *Use your life to be a blessing.* The word "bless" comes from the Old English and means to wish happiness and prosperity or to confer well-being on someone. The perfect way to begin each day is to remind yourself that your life is to be used as a joyful blessing upon others. Here's an exercise to try immediately after waking up but before leaving your home for the day. Offer this simple prayer of blessing: *"This is the day God has made. May I be a source of joyful blessing to everyone I encounter today. May I be the person who sees a need and responds; may I be the person who sees a hurt and tries to heal it."*

In an article titled "The Tattooed Stranger," writer Susan Fahncke tells of driving by a man and his dog on a very, very hot summer day. The man sat on the grass holding up a cardboard sign proclaiming him to be "stuck and hungry" and inviting someone to help. Fahncke pulled her van over pondering the situation. The man had tattoos running up and down both arms and even on his neck. He had a bandanna tied over his head, "biker" style. "Nobody was stopping for him. I could see the other drivers take one look and immediately focus on something else—anything else," she recalls.

As she sat in her van with the air conditioning blowing, this Bible verse suddenly popped into her mind: "Whatever you did for one of the least of these brethren of mine, you did it to me" (Mt 25:40). Fahncke reached into her purse and extracted a ten dollar bill. Her 12-year-old son, Nick, knew right away what she was doing and offered to take the money to the man. Warning him to be careful, she watched as her son approached the homeless man. The stranger was startled and surprised but gladly accepted the gift. When her son came back to the van he said: "Mom, his dog looks so hot and the man really is nice." So, Fahncke knew she had to do more. "Go back and tell him to stay there, that we'll be back in fifteen minutes," she instructed her son. They drove to the nearest store and carefully selected some gifts explaining to her children they couldn't be heavy because the man had to carry whatever they purchased. They settled on two bottles of water— one for the dog and one for the man, a water dish for the dog, some bacon flavored dog food and some people snacks for the man.

Hoping he wasn't a criminal and still somewhat fearful, Fahncke approached the man, gave him their purchases and immediately saw something which made her ashamed of her judgment about him. "I saw tears. He was fighting like a little boy to hold back his tears. How long had it been since someone showed this man kindness?" The stranger stood there like a child before a Christmas tree. When she took out the dog's water dish, the man snatched it out of her hands "as if it were solid gold." Telling her he had no way to give his dog water, he carefully set it down, filling it with the bottled water she bought. Immediately she saw that this "scary" man was "so gentle, so sweet, so humble."

As she drove away, she broke down in tears. Here is her explanation: "Although it seemed as if we had helped him, the man with the tattoos gave us a gift that I will never forget. He taught us that no matter what the outside looks like, inside each of us is a human being deserving of kindness, of compassion, of acceptance . . . tonight and every night I will pray for the gentle man with the tattoos and his dog. And I will hope that God will send more people like him into my life to remind me what's really important."

Seven Further Considerations

1. What do these two quotes have in common: "Joy is the most infallible sign of the presence of God" by Leon Henri Marie Bloy, and "If you have no joy in your religion,

there's a leak in your Christianity somewhere" by Billy Sunday?

2. Describe an experience of joy you have had. What did it feel like? What benefits came from it?

3. What areas of your life need more joy? How can you help that happen?

4. How have you experienced God's creatures, the animals? with fear? with pleasure? with joy? with ambivalence?

5. Do you feel you are a blessing to others? If so, how? If not, why not?

6. Who do you know who is in need of joy? What ways can you help that person reclaim joy in their life?

7. Write this on a card and keep it in a place where you will see it first thing every morning: "What can I do to be more joyful and share joy with everyone I meet?"

HABIT # 3 - PEACE

The Fruit of the Spirit Is . . . Peace

*Great tranquility of heart is his who
cares for neither praise nor blame.*
—Thomas à Kempis

DURING one hot, dry summer in southern California, a brushfire swept through Topanga Canyon, a suburb of Los Angeles, and destroyed 200 homes. Through newspaper reports, Norman Vincent Peale, famed New York City minister and author, realized that one of the homes belonged to a friend of his. Dr. Peale called offering sympathy: "I'm sorry to hear that your house burned down." Expecting that his friend would be traumatized about the fire and his losses, Dr. Peale was astonished when his friend sounded at peace about the tragedy: "Yes, the house did burn down; but my wife and children are safe, and we're all just as healthy as we were before," he said. "All that we lost were some material things—they can be replaced." After thanking Dr. Peale for his call of concern, the man concluded saying: "Call me when I have some real trouble."

Obviously, Dr. Peale's friend knew how to remain serene and peaceful in spite of losing his house and belongings. However, most people would not exhibit such calm composure when facing a similar loss. In fact, many experience life as a series of frenzied, feverish, and frantic events—phones ring, the traffic is heavy, an employer is unreasonable, a customer is rude, a personal or professional crisis arises—all such events seem to squeeze out a sense of personal peace in daily life. "The world is too much with us," wrote poet William Wordsworth in the 1800s. And, Jesus acknowledged that life could become upsetting: "In this world you will have trouble" (Jn 16:33). Yet, life can and should be much more than trials, troubles, and the crowding of activities. It is possible to experience personal peace in spite of life's demands. Jesus also said: "Peace I leave you; my peace I give you . . . Do not let your hearts be troubled and do not be afraid" (Jn 14:27). And the Apostle Paul lists peace as a quality evident in an authentic spiritual life: "The fruit of the spirit is . . . *peace*" (Gal 5:22). Here are some simple suggestions for nurturing tranquility and peace.

• *Memorize The Serenity Prayer.* In 1928 Reinhold Niebuhr became a professor at New York's Union Theological Seminary. Although he would write many books on ethics and theology, he is best remembered for his serenity prayer: "God give us grace to accept with serenity the things that cannot be changed, courage to change the things which should be changed, and the wisdom to distinguish the one from the other." Commit this peace-producing prayer to memory. Recite it daily and whenever you experience inner turmoil. Judy, 37, the owner of a growing but struggling business, has The Serenity Prayer written on a sheet of paper which she has taped on her bathroom mirror. "Having the prayer taped on the mirror is a healing symbol for me. As I wash my face, I also 'wash' away all my anxieties and worries," she says.

• *Take time off from the world.* Remember this wisdom from writer Maya Angelou. "Each person deserves a day away in which no problems are confronted, no solutions searched for. Each of us needs to withdraw from the cares which will not withdraw from us," she writes in her book *Wouldn't Take Nothing for My Journey Now*. Some effective ways of withdrawing temporarily from everyday cares and concerns include spending a few hours in a botanical garden, hiking alone along a mountain trail, or an entire weekend at a spiritual retreat center.

• *Treat all people with dignity.* It's amazing how much inner peace can be cultivated by treating every person we meet with dignity, respect, and honor. Responding to others with courtesy and esteem nurtures peace in yourself and in others. One Sunday morning in 1865, a black man entered a fashionable Episcopalian church in Richmond, Virginia. When Communion was served, he walked down the aisle and knelt at the altar. A rustle of resentment swept the congregation. "How dare he!" was the mood. Episcopalians used the common cup. Then a distinguished layman stood up, stepped forward to the altar and knelt beside the black man. It was Robert E. Lee, former U.S. Confederate General. He spoke these powerful words to the congregation: "All men are brothers in Christ. Have we not all one Father?" Instructed and humbled, the congregation followed his lead.

• *Drop worry.* "Worry is spiritual nearsightedness, a fumbling way of looking at little things, and of magnifying their value," declared theologian and author Anna Robertson Brown. Interestingly, the word worry comes from an old Anglo-Saxon verb *wyrgan* meaning to choke or strangle. Worry is an "emotional weed." Left unchallenged, it spreads quickly strangling and choking the inner life. Worry diminishes an individual by making opponents stronger and problems larger than they really are. Worry drains energy, reduces confidence, heightens fear and positive thought and action. The ancient biblical writer declares: "You . . . worry your way through life and what do you have to show for it?" (Eccl 2:22). Drop worry by beginning to live one day at a time. A good example is television host Kathie Lee Gifford who learned that a disturbed man threatened to harm her. Even from his jail cell where he is serving two life terms for another crime, he continued to write Gifford threatening letters. "From the start I decided I was not going to worry and let this spoil my life," she says. "I have to hand certain things over to God. It's the living out of my faith that makes me a believer. God doesn't just get rid of hardship or suffering, He heals in the midst of it."

• *Begin each day with prayer.* Many people find that morning prayer establishes the right foundation for everything which follows throughout the day. Morning prayer becomes a spiritual anchor which helps us maintain balance and stability, no matter what events emerge. Of course, starting each day with a period of prayer will mean rising a little earlier but even twenty minutes spent in prayer can make a great difference. During that prayer time begin by expressing gratitude to God for your measure of health and wealth. Next, commit the entire day to God with all of its opportunities and obstacles, dreams and disappointments. Affirm that you will use the next twenty-four hours wisely. If you're convinced you're too busy to add prayer time consider this wisdom from St. Francis de

Sales: "Every Christian needs a half hour of prayer each day, except when he is busy, then he needs an hour."

• *Practice hospitality.* Maintain an open house in your heart for other people, especially those who are less fortunate and more distressed; those whose resources are decreasing while their burdens are mounting. Create space in your life for them by responding with kindness, compassion, and practical help. Do whatever you can to fuel hope in their lives. Consider the creative example of Senator Robert Dole and his wife Elizabeth. The couple celebrate their birthdays each year, a week apart, by hosting a party for a roomful of underprivileged teenagers. Although the Doles have very hectic, packed schedules, they make time for such acts of kindness. The Doles consider these kinds of charitable activities extremely important because they directly help others, and indirectly, result in nation building. The human heart always glows with satisfaction and peace whenever we reach out and help another person.

• *Be a good neighbor.* "Love your neighbor as yourself," Jesus commanded (Mt 22:39). Offer your assistance to people in the neighborhood. Lucy, 33, a suburban Chicago mother of two pre-schoolers, does grocery shopping for an elderly couple who live on her street. "It only takes me an hour a week and I feel so good about doing it," she says. Sometimes Lucy drives the elderly couple for medical appointments. "By doing this I've made two terrific friends. While my driving and errand running does help them out, I feel I've benefited much more. I can't begin to describe how much joy doing this has brought into my life."

• *Avoid self-pity.* Do not be seduced by the temptation to feel sorry for yourself because you don't have a better job, make more money, have a larger house, drive a newer car or aren't successful as your neighbor. Minister and author Charles Swindoll makes this observation: "Self-pity . . . cuddle and nurse it as an infant and you'll have on your hands in a brief period of time a beast, a monster, a raging, coarse brute that will spread the poison of bitterness and paranoia throughout your system." If you are tempted to feel sorry for yourself, try eliminating self-pity by adopting a technique which worked for the late actress Joan Blondell. She used a common kitchen timer to pull herself out of a self-pity session. "I set the timer for six and one-half minutes to be lonely, and twenty-two minutes to feel sorry for myself. And then when the bell rings, I take a shower, or a walk, or a swim, or I cook something—and think about something else," she explained.

Ultimately, peace and serenity are most likely to be present when we allow our lives to mirror the peace of God. Gerhard Tersteegen, the 18th century German mystic accurately observed: "God is a tranquil being and abides in tranquil eternity. So must your spirit become a tranquil and clear little pool, wherein the serene light of God can be mirrored."

Seven Further Considerations

1. Think back to a traumatic time in your life. Was it filled only with tension and anxiety or were you able to experience moments of peace?

2. Why has The Serenity Prayer become so popular? In what area of your life can you put this prayer into practice?

3. How do you take time away from the world? If you are not in the habit of doing this from time to time, what are some ways you could do this?

4. Do you feel daily prayer and meditation are important? How can they be more prominent in your life?

5. Would others view you as a good neighbor? In what ways do you try to bring a calming and peaceful presence where you live?

6. What are some ways you have tried to mirror the peace of God?

7. Identify some people you know who are peaceful. What is it about them that makes them peaceful? How can you make those qualities your own?

HABIT #4 - PATIENCE

The Fruit of the Spirit Is . . . Patience

Adopt the pace of nature;
her secret is patience.
—Ralph Waldo Emerson

NEARLY 600 years before the birth of Christ, a slave named Aesop who lived in Greece, told the tale of the crow. The bird was nearly dying from thirst when she found a tall pitcher that was half full of water. However, when she tried to drink from the pitcher she discovered sadly that her beak was not long enough to reach the water deep down inside the pitcher. She tried, with all her might, to knock the pitcher over so she could drink the spilled water but the pitcher was too heavy for her to budge.

Desperate to quench her thirst and, ultimately, save her life, the crow came up with a plan. She picked up a little rock in her beak and dropped it into the pitcher. The water rose a tiny bit in the pitcher. Next she dropped in another pebble. The water rose again a little more. One by one she dropped hundreds of pebbles into the big, deep pitcher until the water rose nearly to the top. As she took a nice long drink, she told herself, "Patience works where force fails."

Aesop was using the story of the crow to provide important lessons for living. The most obvious lesson, of course, is that patience is critical for managing and overcoming difficulty. Yet, this vital life skill is profoundly absent in many parts of our society. We are people who have lost the virtue of patience. Too many men and women are impatient on our highways and streets, resulting in increasing incidents of road rage. Too many men and women are impatient in our stores, mistreating clerks. Too many men and women are impatient even among family and friends, lashing out at one another. There is an epidemic of impatience in our culture. Sensing this trait in humanity, the Bible repeatedly exhorts people of faith to exercise patience and to continuously cultivate this virtue. The Apostle Paul identifies patience as a key virtue of the spiritual life: "The fruit of the Spirit is love, joy, peace, *patience . . .*" (Gal 5:22). Jesus taught: "By standing firm, you will gain life." Advising Christians in Rome, Paul wrote: "Be joyful in hope, patient in affliction, persevering in prayer" (Rom 12:12). The Old Testament prophet Habakkuk reinforces the importance of patience, advising: "Though it linger, wait for it" (Hab 2:3). Behind those statements is this understanding: patience is the ability to wait and work for a successful outcome. The virtue of patience contains seeds of tolerance, restraint, and perseverance. Without patience, we run the risk of sabotaging our life goals and dreams. Here are five strategies for developing patience.

1. *Be flexible.* Meetings may not start on time. Friends may be late for lunch. Road construction may delay you. Projects may have setbacks. Deadlines may be missed. These types of events are common in life. A rigid approach to them only serves to fuel frustration and impatience. Be flexible. Flow with the unexpected and unexpected benefits will come your way. Author Lin Morel tells of giving a speech for a women's organization. Along with making a presentation, Morel was offered

a table on which to sell her products. "The speech was a great success, the table another story!" she recalls. Unknown to her, the organization planned a lengthy business meeting immediately following her speech preventing those in the audience from browsing through the products she displayed on the table. As the meeting dragged on, Morel wanted to simply remove her products and leave but knew the noise she made packing up would be disruptive. "I could see no graceful way out of my dilemma. So, I waited and waited, and waited some more. I watched the audience begin to trickle out as the night deepened, morning beckoned, and the meeting droned on."

She became discouraged about selling anything so she challenged her negative attitude telling herself: "The night isn't over until you're home. Be patient. Wait and see." Events unfolded in a surprising way for her. "Sure enough, patience was the name of the game," she recalls. As the meeting ended, the president reminded the audience to stop by her table. "A short time later, I sold everything I brought with me, handed out information and reconnected with my audience. I was the last one to leave the room, satchel empty, pockets full."

2. *Allow life to be your instructor in patience.* Let the events of daily life, whether those are large or small, be the source of your education in patience. For example:

- Be patient when you are mistreated.
- Be patient when you don't know why.
- Be patient when you must wait.
- Be patient when you are sick.
- Be patient when you've been gossiped about.

- Be patient when you lose a job.
- Be patient when your children frustrate you.
- Be patient when a friend fails to come through.
- Be patient when someone turns against you.
- Be patient when criticized.
- Be patient when encountering resistance.
- Be patient when job hunting.
- Be patient with step children.

Patience produces peace of mind according to the 14th Dalai Lama (born 1934): "Patient forbearance is the quality which enables us to prevent negative thoughts and emotions from taking hold of us. It safeguards our peace of mind in the face of adversity."

3. *Change the flow of your thinking.* "There is a river whose streams bring joy to the city of God," writes the psalmist (Ps 46:5). In that passage, the river represents the flow of our thoughts and often we need to change the flow of our thinking in order to develop great patience and reap the benefits. In viewing any situation, we can think in ways that exasperate us or in ways that exhilarate us. Consider the experience of minister and author John C. Maxwell when he and his wife, Margaret, took fifty people to tour the Holy Land. "Margaret and I are super planners, so in the space of a week, we saw more sights than many thought was humanly possible. But by the time we were headed back home, everyone was exhausted," he recalls. When the group arrived in Paris from Tel Aviv at midmorning, an agent told them their flight to New York was cancelled due to a major snowstorm on the Atlantic coast.

"Nothing is going in or out for the next twenty-four hours," the agent explained.

Immediately Maxwell and his wife sensed disappointment and frustration among the group. "Many who were traveling with us were older and had never been out of the United States before that trip. Previous departures from the planned itinerary had upset some of them. The major break in our travel plans was likely to send them into panic." Knowing they had to act, Maxwell and his wife said to the group: "This is great. We've got an awesome opportunity here," and announced they were going to take a tour of Paris. Quickly they arranged for a bus, loaded the group, and gave them a whirlwind tour of Paris. "Take lots of pictures," the Maxwells kept saying. "You'll want to show everyone when you get home how you got an extra trip to Paris." Soon everyone was delighted with this unexpected opportunity. They even spotted pop singer Madonna coming out of the Louvre surrounded by bodyguards. Everyone took pictures of her. "After we got home, our people had meaningful memories of Israel and the awe-inspiring places there. But their favorite story was about their one-day side trip to Paris," he says.

4. *Live in the present moment.* Much of our impatience is due to our inability to be accepting and comfortable with events and situations as they present themselves. Cherie Carter-Scott, Ph.D., and author of *If Life Is a Game, These Are the Rules*, explains: "Living in the present brings the one thing most people spend their lives striving to achieve: peace. Relaxing into the present moment puts you in the mental and physical state of calm, quiet, and tranquility and finally gets us

off the here-but-gotta-get-there treadmill. If you are in the moment of doing whatever you are doing, then there is not time to examine the gap between your expectation and the reality of how things are, or between where you are and where you think you should be. You are too busy being in the moment to analyze it and find fault with it."

5. *Practice patience with yourself.* Reversing the habit of impatience can take time. Rather than berate yourself when you have a relapse into impatience, embrace the biblical teaching to "throw off everything that weighs us down" (Heb 12:1). Throw off any feelings of guilt over a moment of impatience and continue working at it. Here's a lesson via a monk who was very impatient. The more he tried to be patient, the more impatient he became. Consequently, he decided that he had to get away completely so he could learn patience. So he built himself a little hut deep in the woods, far away from any of the villages. Years later, a man was traveling in those woods and met him. The man was amazed to find anyone living alone and so far away from others. He asked the monk why he was there all by himself. The monk explained he was there to learn to be patient. "And how long have you been here by yourself?" the traveler asked. The monk told him he had been there seven years. Stunned, the traveler asked, "If there is no one around to bother you, how will you know when you are patient?" At that point, the monk became irritated with answering questions and shouted: "Get away from me, I have no time for you."

The story of that monk offers this lesson: don't allow yourself to become overly frustrated and quickly defeated in your effort to be a more patient person. Expect relapses but continue working to cultivate this virtue. Remember to be patient with yourself. If you become discouraged because you were impatient, recall this wisdom from author Eknath Easwaran: "Patience can't be acquired overnight. It is just like building up a muscle. Every day you need to work on it."

Seven Further Considerations

1. Who is the most patient person you know? What makes him or her that way?

2. What areas of your life need more flexibility?

3. Which life issues are you dealing with right now that can teach you patience?

4. How does your thinking contribute to patience or impatience?

5. What would it mean for you to live in the present moment?

6.   Where in your life do you need to be more patient?

7. What is the meaning of this quote by Gandhi: "Patience means self-suffering"?

HABIT #5 - KINDNESS

The Fruit of the Spirit Is . . . Kindness

*Love and kindness are never wasted. They always
make a difference. They bless the one who receives
them, and they bless you the giver.*
—Barbara De Angelis

A woman recently wrote an advice columnist to share
how a simple act of kindness prompted her to seriously
change her lifestyle. Signing herself only as "Slimming Fast in
Florida," the woman explained she is one of those "oversized"
people who more than fills an airline seat. While on an airplane
which was filled nearly to capacity, a "good looking gentleman" sat down in the seat directly beside her. He greeted her
with a friendly "good morning" and flashed a warm smile. As
he buckled his seat belt, he said to the woman: "I always feel
cramped in these seats. Would you mind if I raised the armrest
between us?" Slimming Fast in Florida knew "he didn't feel
cramped. He wanted to make sure I was more comfortable."

During the flight the man complimented the woman on
her hairstyle and the "lovely dress" she was wearing. "His
remarks had a lasting effect on me," the woman concluded in
her letter. "Since that flight, I have lost 23 pounds, thanks to a
gentleman who didn't scowl at an overweight woman, but
instead, made her feel attractive."

There is an important lesson to be gleaned from the
encounter between an "oversized" woman and her gentle

traveling companion and it is this: a small act of kindness can have a large impact. "A kind heart is a fountain of gladness, making everything in its vicinity freshen into smiles," observed author Washington Irving. So important is kindness in daily living that the Talmud—a series of Rabbinical writings put together from the first through sixth centuries of the Common Era—declares: "Deeds of kindness are equal in weight to all the commandments." St. Paul, another Jewish writer, identified kindness as a vital part of any spiritual life: "The fruit of the spirit is ... *kindness*" (Gal 5:22). Here are some ways to bring back kindness.

1. *Begin by reminding yourself that kindness is in short supply.* Psychiatrist Edward M. Hallowell, author of *Human Moments*, describes our times as a "culture of rancor" in which people are constantly "argumentative, attacking, loud, opinionated, self-righteous, cocksure, divisive, disconnected." Dr. Hallowell offers this additional observation: "Sometimes when I'm stopped at a traffic light, I look at the faces of the drivers passing by in front of me. So many look so grumpy! I know sitting in traffic is not exactly happy time, but I still think these faces represent a national problem: We simply do not get enough positive human contact in our daily life. Emotionally we're running on fumes, if not on empty." Do your part to offset this dilemma by being a person who is kind in thought, word, and deed. Apply daily, the exhortation of scripture to: "Clothe yourselves with compassion, kindness . . . " (Col 3:12).

2. *Make kindness your daily priority.* J. M. Barrie, author of *Peter Pan* and other works suggested: "Shall we make a new rule of life from tonight: always to try to be a little kinder than

is necessary." No matter what you do or where you live commit to making kindness a priority in daily life. Whether you are a busy professional or engaged in a trade or work as a homemaker, make it a daily goal to speak and act kindly. "Bring back pleasant conversation, eye contact with strangers, family dinners, and an ability to praise people and thank them for what they do right," advises Dr. Hallowell.

The biblical leader, Moses, was one who practiced daily kindness and made it a priority of his life. In Exodus 2:16ff, an incident is related in which seven women approached a desert well in order to water a flock of animals. Nearby, were a group of shepherds, who, upon seeing the defenseless women, attacked and drove them away. It was Moses who came to their rescue. He not only persuaded the shepherds to leave the women alone, but then helped the women water their flock and remained at their side to ensure their safety and the completion of their task.

3. *Offer the kindness of gratitude.* Express gratitude for those many people who make your life a little more comfortable and pleasant. Before going on your way, pause to smile and thank the store clerk, the bank teller, the postal carrier, the automobile mechanic, the plumber, etc. Your kind expression may be a rare word of appreciation heard by that person. Consider the lesson learned by Watsonville, California resident Myrna Vermette, who sat down and wrote a thank-you note to her dentist. "I was so grateful for the good job he had done, and for the minimal pain it had caused me, that I had to write."

A few months later she developed an abscessed tooth and found herself at the dentist's office once again. To her astonishment, she spotted her letter, framed in glass, hanging on the wall. "Your kind words meant so much to me," the dentist explained, "I wanted to be reminded of them every day."

4. *Let these seed thoughts of kindness grow in your soul.* Deepen your desire to be kind and activate your will by reflecting on these words of wisdom concerning kindness:

- "Three things in human life are important. The first is to be kind. The second is to be kind. And the third is to be kind."   —Henry James

- "It's easy to criticize others and make them feel unwanted. Anyone can do it. What takes effort and skill is picking them up and making them feel good."

    —Rabbi Nachman of Breslov, a Hasidic master.

- "In this world, you must be a bit too kind in order to be kind enough."   —Pierre Marivaux

- "When I was young, I used to admire intelligent people; as I grow older, I admire kind people."

    —Rabbi Abraham Joshua Heschel,
    writing near the end of his life.

And, add to those inspirational sentences, these calls from the writers of Scripture:

- Romans 12:10—"Love one another with genuine affection. Esteem others above yourselves."

- 1 Corinthians 13:4 — "Love is patient, love is kind . . ."

- 2 Peter 1:5 - 7 — "Make every effort to add to your faith . . . kindness."

5. *Practice kindness in your neighborhood.* "While the spirit of neighborliness was important on the frontier because neigh-

bors were so few, it is even more important now because our neighbors are so many," is the wise observation of Lady Bird Johnson, wife of former U.S. President Lyndon Johnson. Be considerate of your neighbors and act kindly toward them. When Microsoft founder Bill Gates and his wife Melinda were building their enormous 65,000-foot home in the small community of Medina, Washington, they knew the massive construction effort would be disruptive to their neighbors. Before any construction workers and equipment were in place, the couple invited neighbors to their old home. There they showed people their construction plans and answered questions which neighbors had. Then, the Gates' published a newsletter about the project and paid to have their neighbors' cars washed when construction dust was a problem. Finally, when the house was completed, they threw two parties. The first was for the construction crew and the second party was for the neighbors. As a result of the Gates' kindness, several neighbors have campaigned to establish a Bill and Melinda Gates day in the community. "They deserve respect because they've earned it," say the Gates' neighbors.

6. *Piggy back with others who are kind.* Support others when you see them engaged in kind actions. Don't allow yourself to be a mere spectator of kindness but plunge into the arena and join them. In 1948, Veronica Bradway was a young Roman Catholic sister working with others in her religious order, teaching children of migrant workers. One cold day, a mother reluctantly approached the sisters asking if they could obtain a blanket. Her family of four were sharing one blanket padded with newspapers to sleep under, the mother explained. The

next day, armed with less than six dollars, the sisters made their way to a local department store. The owner began to show them beautiful blankets but the sisters told him they were more interested in warmth than beauty. So, the owner pulled out some Army blankets. They were slightly defective, having a small hole at one corner where a cord held a dozen blankets together. "When he found out what we wanted the blanket for, he gave us the entire dozen, and another dozen besides," Sister Veronica recalls. "Then he asked how many children were in that small migrant camp. He went through his store, pulling out sweaters of all sizes, and toys of all kinds."

7. *Put yourself on a kindness team.* Mia Daveline, a 36-year-old secretary asked her employer for a month off with pay to care for her husband, Kerry, who was suffering from stage four melanoma. It couldn't be done, she was told. Co-worker Alicia Rodriguez asked other workers if they'd give up vacation or sick time for Mia, as she planned to do. Quickly, a kindness team was formed and seventeen workers donated 20 days, with pay. Factoring in weekends, Mia had her paid month off to help her husband.

Finally, as you act to bring back kindness remind yourself that anyone can be kind and everyone must be kind. A perfect time to begin bringing back kindness is the present moment. So as you go through your day, offer others a word of thanks, a nod of approval, a sentence of appreciation, a surprise compliment, a warm smile.

Seven Further Considerations

1. What act of kindness has touched and deepened your life?

2. Do you believe there is a shortage of kindness? Why is this?

3. Why do sages and writers of scripture stress the importance of kindness in daily life?

4. How have you witnessed or experienced kindness from a neighbor?

5. Albert Schweitzer wrote: "The sun makes ice melt; kindness causes misunderstanding, mistrust, and hostility to evaporate." Think about his words and discuss them with some friends.

6. Identify people in your neighborhood, workplace, or church with whom you could form a kindness team.

7. Discuss the wisdom of this statement by Rabbi Abraham Joshua Heschel: "When I was young, I used to admire intelligent people; as I grow older, I admire kind people."

HABIT #6 - GOODNESS

The Fruit of the Spirit Is . . . Goodness

Goodness is something so simple;
always live for others, never to seek one's
advantage. —Dag Hammarskjold

SEVERAL years ago, Collin Perry was living the "American Dream." He had a thriving construction business, a comfortable home, two new cars, a sailboat, and was happily married. Then the business climate soured and high interest rates eroded his savings. He lay awake at night in a cold sweat knowing he couldn't make ends meet. Just when he thought things couldn't get worse, his wife declared she wanted a divorce.

With no idea what to do next, he went to his sailboat and literally began to "sail off into the sunset." He started by following the coastline from Connecticut to Florida but somewhere off the New Jersey coast he turned due east, straight out to sea. Hours later he stood on the stern rail watching the dark Atlantic and thought to himself: "How easy it would be to let the water take me!"

Suddenly the boat plummeted knocking him off balance. Desperately, he grabbed the rail and clung for dear life. As his feet were dragged through the icy brine he managed to pull himself back on board. Shaken, he realized that he did not truly want to die. "From that moment, I knew I had to see things through. My old life was gone. Somehow I'd have to build a new one," he recalls.

Although Collin Perry gained a new appreciation for life through his adversity, it is not necessary to experience life's trials and troubles in order to feel good about living. Daily, we can cultivate spiritual approaches to life that will bring us optimal fulfillment and satisfaction. Doing so means we will share in the delight of the psalmist—*This is the day the Lord has made; let us exult and rejoice in it* (Ps 118:24). Goodness is also identified by the Apostle Paul as an element of a spiritual life: "The fruit of the spirit is . . . *goodness*" (Gal 5:22). Consider these eight simple guidelines for feeling good *every day*.

1. *Begin each day with a blessing.* That advice is offered by Charlotte Davis Kasl, Ph.D., a Quaker psychologist and healer. In her book, *Finding Joy: 101 Ways to Free Your Spirit,* she writes: "A wonderful way to start the day is to bless it." Dr. Davis Kasl offers these examples:

> Blessings on this day, may I make it special in some way.
>
> Blessings on my life, may I treat it with love and care.
>
> Blessings on all people, may I see the goodness in everyone.
>
> Blessings on nature, may I notice its beauty and wonder.
>
> Blessings on the truth, may it be my constant companion.

2. *Be honorable in all your dealings.* From the Jewish tradition there is a story about a rabbi who purchased a camel from a trader at the bazaar. When the rabbi arrived home, he discovered a valuable diamond in the camel's saddlebag. He immediately returned the diamond to its rightful owner and

said, "Sir, I purchased a camel, not a diamond; the diamond is still rightfully yours." The moral of that story is clear: we have an obligation to be honorable in all our dealings.

Feeling good about yourself requires personal integrity. Maintain the highest ethical standards. Keep your word. Treat others fairly. Virtues like those open the door to deep satisfaction with life

3. *Use your influence to help someone else.* A woman simply signed as 'Carol' wrote to an advice columnist to share not a problem but a joy which surprised her life. In the early 1990s the woman saw the movie, *Crazy People,* starring Dudley Moore. The film was about people with mental illness who banded together to become productive citizens in their community. The writer felt the movie sent a clear and positive message to the public about people struggling with mental illness. "Since I suffer from clinical depression and have for most of my life, I wrote a letter to Dudley Moore telling him how much this picture helped me," she says. To her surprise, a few months later, her phone rang and she heard: "May I speak to Carol? This is Dudley Moore calling." The actor called simply to express support for Carol in her struggle with clinical depression. Carol described the actor as modest, sincere, and extremely caring. "I can't tell you what a big help it was knowing that someone of his fame still cares for those who fight a daily battle with mental illness. It made my day," she concluded.

It is worth recalling Jesus' statement: "You are the salt of the earth" (Mt 5:13). Those words are a reminder that we have influence. Like salt, we flavor life by what we say and do.

While most of us are not famous actors and actresses, all of us have influence over someone—a child, a spouse, a relative, a friend, a neighbor. Perhaps, because of our profession or standing in a community, we have a larger sphere of influence. Whatever the case, we should, like Dudley Moore, use our influence to help others.

4. *Let time be a tool, not a tyrant.* "Take care to live as intelligent people," advised St. Paul (Eph 5:15). People who are extremely busy, racing from one activity to another hour after hour, often express frustration over the hectic pace of their lives. On the other hand, there are people who feel they have too much time and spend their hours "killing" time or "filling" time with unfulfilling activities. These individuals often express boredom and discouragement with their lives. In each case, both the frustration and the discouragement can be eliminated by learning to make time a tool rather than letting it be a tyrant. "You must learn to regard the clock as an artist regards his materials; not as a whip but as a paintbrush to add beauty to the picture you are creating," says Dr. Robert Anthony, author of *The Ultimate Secrets of Total Self-Confidence.*

He advises that time be used for specific purposes and clear objectives which enhance the quality of your life. Simply setting priorities is the key that opens the door to effective use of time. "Get into the habit of writing down each night before retiring, the six most important things you want to do the next day," he recommends. "After you list these, put them in their order or priority. As you get those things done you set out to do, you will be filled with a great sense of accomplishment.

Each project you complete will make the next seem easier. And success will follow success."

The Dalai Lama has a time philosophy worthy of imitating: "Every day, think as you wake up, today I am fortunate to be alive. I have a precious human life; I am not going to waste it. I am going to use all my energies to develop myself, to expand my heart out to others; to achieve enlightenment for the benefit of all beings. I am going to have kind thoughts towards others; I am not going to get angry or think badly about others. I am going to benefit others as much as I can."

5. *Do your part to keep the earth clean.* Here's a good tip from Sadie and Bessie Delany who were 105 and 103 years of age when they published their first book, *Having Our Say* (1993). In 1994 they authored *The Delany Sisters' Book of Everyday Wisdom.* There they wrote: "It's strange how many people don't seem to care about anyone else. For example, we can't get over the litter on the ground in New York City. People eat a sandwich, and they throw the wrapper on the ground. You might think that's a little thing to be provoked about, but it's not a little thing. It shows a lot about the character of the person. By throwing something on the ground, that person is saying he's thoughtless about others."

The lesson: everyone has an obligation to keep the earth clean. Not only should we avoid littering but we ought to make it a habit to pick up litter whenever possible. A good friend of mine made an indelible impression on me as we were jogging along the boardwalk in Virginia Beach. He interrupted his run several times to quickly bend down and pick up empty soda cans that had been carelessly thrown on the ground. As he continued jogging, he dropped the items into garbage containers that were spaced all along the boardwalk.

6. *Build and maintain a support network.* Don't be a soloist in life. Don't go it alone. Connect with others in common causes. Join civic organizations, church groups, self-help and professional associations. Tap into the healing network of family and friends, neighbors, and colleagues so that when stressful, difficult times come, you will have supportive people all around.

7. *Practice forgiveness daily.* Almost daily, life brings us all sorts of slights and hurts. As we learn to forgive and forget the lesser slights of life each day, we are more able to extend forgiveness over larger, more painful issues. Withholding forgiveness while harboring resentment and anger simply pollutes life. One who recommends practicing forgiveness is Redford Williams, M.D., an expert on heart health and author of *The Trusting Heart: Great News About Type A Behavior.* Dr. Williams says: "By letting go of the resentment and relinquishing the goal of retribution, you may find that the weight of anger lifts from your shoulders, easing your pain, and also helping you to forget the wrong."

If you find it difficult to forgive, perhaps this encounter from minister and author Robert H. Schuller can help you become a better forgiver. On one occasion he was counseling a woman who was extremely angry and bitter over her divorce. When Dr. Schuller advised her to forgive her ex-husband, the woman became agitated with him. Dr. Schuller suggested she was confusing forgiveness with reconciliation. He described the forgiveness process this way: "Forgiveness does not mean you have to approve of his behavior! You could never do that!

But forgiveness does mean you are going to put it behind you—and yes—in practical terms—forget it! Which means you'll bury the hatchet and not leave the handle above the ground! But to forgive and forget does not mean you have to have a restored relationship! You don't even need to become friends. You just have to stop being enemies!"

8. *Strive to be a true friend.* Finally, be guided by this wisdom from William Penn: "A true friend unbosoms freely, advises justly, assists readily, adventures boldly, takes all patiently, defends courageously, and continues a friend unchangeably." Being a faithful, true friend always results in feeling good about ourselves and our lives.

Seven Further Considerations

1. Why do you think goodness is listed as a spiritual fruit?

2. It has been said that when we help someone else we end up also helping ourselves. Do you agree with this concept?

3. How does being honorable lead to feeling good?

4. Describe someone you know who clearly exhibits this fruit of the spirit. What can you learn from this individual?

5. Discuss this quotation from Edward George Bulwer-Lytton: "A good heart is better than all the heads in the world."

6. In what ways does a forgiving heart open the way for feeling good?

7.   Think and talk about this observation from John Wooden: "You can't live a perfect day without doing something for someone who will never be able to repay you."

HABIT #7 - FAITHFULNESS

The Fruit of the Spirit Is . . . Faithfulness

Faithfulness in little things is a big thing.

—St. John Chrysostom

IN the eleventh century, Henry III, king of Germany, became dissatisfied with court life and the pressures of the monarchy. Unlike many rulers, Henry was a deeply spiritual individual whose faith guided his daily life and rule. Therefore he made a visit to Prior Richard, the leader of a local monastery, asking to be received as a contemplative. His wish, Henry explained, was to spend the rest of his life in the monastery.

"Your Majesty," responded Prior Richard, "do you understand that the pledge here is one of obedience? That will be hard because you have been a King."

"I understand," said Henry. "The rest of my life I will be obedient to you, as Christ leads you."

"Then I will tell you what to do," said the Prior. "Go back to your throne and serve faithfully in the place where God has put you."

Undoubtedly Prior Richard's advice to Henry III was surprising and perhaps even disappointing to the King. Yet, the prior touched upon an important theme of the spiritual *life—faithfulness*. When we grow weary of our roles and responsibilities, when the temptation to give up and quit is great, when we would prefer to flee rather than face the challenges of daily living, we should first remind ourselves that God calls us to be faithful.

Of course, there are times when we should cut our losses, detach from impossible situations, and move forward in life. However, before doing that we need to remember that there are times when God places us in certain situations and that God expects us to be dependable, loyal, conscientious. This is true when marriage is hard, parenting difficult, work challenging. It is true whether we are lay or clergy, workers or homemakers, plumbers or executives, entrepreneurs or employees.

Across the ages, saints and mystics have declared that faithfulness is an important spiritual discipline. "Faithfulness in little things is a big thing," noted St. John Chrysostom, the great 4th century preacher. Evelyn Underhill, a 20th century British spiritual writer said: "Faithfulness is consecration in overalls."

Faithfulness is also a common biblical theme. Scripture consistently reminds us not to give up the battle or to take the easy way out. Some examples include Galatians 6:9: "Let us never grow weary in doing good, for if we do not give up, we will reap a harvest in due time." James 1:12: "Blessed is the man who perseveres when he is tested, because when he has been proven, he will receive the crown of life that God has promised to those who love him." Faithfulness—the qualities of commitment, dedication, loyalty are the hallmarks of spiritual maturity. It is cited by the Apostle Paul as a spiritual fruit: "The fruit of the spirit is . . . *faithfulness*" (Gal 5:22). Here are some arenas of life where faithfulness is vital.

• *Faithful in our work.* Even though many jobs are not high-paying or glamorous, we can add dignity to the task and meaning to our lives by doing the work to the best of our abilities. Martin Luther King, Jr. said: "If a man is called to be a streetsweeeper, he should sweep streets even as Michelangelo painted, or Beethoven composed music, or Shakespeare wrote poetry. He should sweep streets so well that all the hosts of heaven and earth will pause to say: 'Here lived a great streetsweeper who did his job well.' "

Currently the president of Brown University, Ruth Simmons had been the president of Smith College, one of the country's most prestigious institutions of higher learning for women. It was an incredible achievement for a woman who is the great-great-granddaughter of slaves. Simmons began her journey to Smith on a cotton farm in Grapeland, Texas, where her parents were sharecroppers. Later they moved to an impoverished section of Houston where her father found work in a factory and her mother scrubbed floors for white families. When asked how such humble beginnings led to a career at the top of academia, Simmons answers: "I had a remarkable mother. She would sometimes take me with her to work when I was a little girl, and the thing I remember vividly is how good she was at what she did. She was very demanding in terms of her own work. 'Do it well, do it thoroughly, whatever you do,' she'd say." Simmons' mother continues to influence her work even as president of Smith College. "I know the Smith Board of Trustees thinks I'm trying to live up to the standards they set for me, and that's okay," she says. But, Simmons has a higher standard: "Every day that I'm here I try to be the kind of person my mother wanted me to be."

• *Faithful in prayer.* "More things are wrought by prayer than this world dreams of," noted poet Alfred Tennyson. And in the Gospel of Luke we are told that Jesus used a parable to convey this one important lesson for his followers: "That they should always pray and not give up" (Lk 18:1). These insights about prayer should nudge us to do a careful examination of conscience—Do we truly believe in the power of prayer? How often do we pray? Are we sincere and serious in our praying? Do we include those around us who are hurting? Larry Dossey, M.D, is an unusual physician because he employs the power of prayer in his medical practice. An incident early in his career alerted him to the power of prayer. At the time Dossey was doing his residency training in Dallas, Texas. There he had a patient with terminal cancer in both lungs. "I advised him on what therapy was available and what little I thought it would do. Rightly enough, he opted for no treatment," Dossey recalls in his book *Healing Words.* "Yet whenever I stopped by his hospital bedside, he was surrounded by visitors from his church, singing and praying. *Good thing,* I thought, *because soon they'll be singing and praying at his funeral."*

A year later he was working elsewhere when a colleague from Dallas called asking if Dossey wanted to see his old patient. "See him? I couldn't believe he was still alive," Dossey remembered thinking. Studying his chest X rays, Dossey was stunned. The man's lungs were completely clear—there was absolutely no sign of cancer. The radiologist, looking over Dossey's shoulder commented that the man's therapy was remarkable. *"Therapy?* I thought. *There wasn't any—unless you consider prayer."*

• *Faithful in our commitments to others.* It is always disappointing and disillusioning when someone we have counted on does not come through. It is a sad fact of life that not everyone who volunteers for a task completes it. Not everyone who says he or she will do a job actually does it. Many find reasons and excuses not to complete their commitments. Yet, life is pleasantly flavored by those who are dependable—those who fulfill what they agreed to do even when it requires unexpected sacrifices. In 1947, a professor at the University of Chicago, Subrahmanyan Chandrasekhar, Ph.D., was scheduled to teach an advanced seminar in astrophysics. At the time he was living in Wisconsin, doing research at the Yerkes Astronomical Observatory. He planned to commute twice a week for the class, even though it would be held during the harsh winter months.

But only two students signed up for the class. People expected Dr. Chandrasekhar to cancel rather than waste his time on such a small class. But for the sake of two students, he taught the class, commuting 100 miles round trip over back country roads in the dead of winter. His students, Chen Ning Yang and Tsung-Dao Lee, did their homework. Ten years later, they both won the Nobel Prize for physics. Dr. Chandrasekhar won the same prize in 1983. The professor demonstrated the rare and remarkable virtue of faithfulness: he could be counted on.

• *Faithful to ourselves.* Another arena of life where many experience faithfulness failure is to themselves. When life sends a setback or delivers a harsh blow, too many people give up on themselves. Rather than remain faithful to their dreams and aspirations, they allow themselves a cheap resignation to fate. Rather than look at what remains, they focus bitterly on what has been lost. In so doing, they often become cynical and leave latent talents undeveloped. However, there are those who do not choose the path of least resistance when faced with major life challenges.

Consider the glowing example of Sarah Reinertsen who was born in 1975 with only part of her left leg. Even that had to be removed to the hip when she was 7. In spite of being an amputee, the little girl was determined to pursue her interest in athletics. When she was 12, Sarah began working long, hard hours with her track and field coach. Together they developed a new way for an amputee to run. Until then, most above-the-knee amputee runners ran by hopping twice on their good leg, then kicking their artificial leg forward. Sarah was the first to use the new step-over-step method in competitions. She runs by taking one step with each leg, the same way people with two legs run. That new method allows above-the-knee amputees to run much faster. Sara Reinertsen became the fastest female above-the-knee-amputee runner in the world. Because she was faithful to herself, she held world records in the 100-meter and 200-meter runs.

Finally, when we grow weary of daily responsibilities and are tempted, like Henry III, to abandon our post, it can help to review these words from the writer John Oxenham:

> *Is your place a small place?*
> *Tend it with care!—He set you there.*
> *Is your place a large place?*
> *Tend it with care!—He set you there.*

Whate'er your place, it is
Not yours alone, but His
Who set you there.

Seven Further Considerations

1. How does the quote from St. John Chrysostom— "Faithfulness in little things is a big thing"—apply to your life?

2. Think of an individual who most exemplifies faithfulness. What are his or her faithfulness traits?

3. What areas of your life reflect a lack of faithfulness? What corrective steps could you take?

4. Do you know someone who is struggling with a life challenge? How could you pray for their well being consistently and faithfully?

5. Why did Mother Teresa of Calcutta say this: "I do not pray for success; I ask for faithfulness"?

6. Who, in your life, needs more commitment and faithfulness from you?

7. What are the times in your life when you need to dig deeper and be faithful to yourself, your dreams, your hopes?

HABIT #8 - GENTLENESS

The Fruit of the Spirit Is . . . Gentleness

Nothing is so strong as gentleness,
nothing so gentle as real strength.
　　　　　　　　　　—St. Francis de Sales

IN 1921 when Lewis Lawes became warden at Sing Sing Prison (now Ossining Correctional Facility) in Ossining, NY it had a reputation for being the toughest place of confinement in the country's prison system. The most notorious and incorrigible criminals were sent off to this severe and unforgiving place. But, when Warden Lawes retired twenty years later, the prison had become a model for the humane treatment of prisoners and for the development of programs designed to rehabilitate prisoners. Those who studied the system said credit for the change belonged to Warden Lawes whose novel penal administrative policies emphasized a rehabilitative role for prisons. Warden Lawes instituted such reforms as the establishment of theatricals, film showings, athletics, and provision of radio earphones for each cell. He also required all inmates to wear the same kind of uniform in order to blur distinctions of wealth and outside status.

Yet when asked about his success and the transformation of the prison Warden Lawes said: "I owe it all to my wonderful wife, Catherine, who is buried outside the prison walls." Catherine Lawes was a young mother with three small children when her husband became the warden. Although many people warned her never to set foot inside the prison walls,

Catherine disregarded their advice. When the first prison basketball game was held, she went, bringing her three small children and sat in the stands with inmates. Upon learning that one convicted murderer was blind, she taught him Braille. When she found a hearing impaired prisoner, she learned how to use sign language in order to communicate with him.

Quietly and lovingly she worked with prisoners from 1921 until 1937. Then, she was killed in a car accident. The next morning Lewis Lawes didn't come to work so the acting warden took his place. Instantly the entire prison population knew something was wrong. The following day Catherine Lawes body lay in state at her home, three-quarters of a mile from the prison. As the acting warden toured the prison that morning he was shocked to see a large crowd of the toughest, most hardened prisoners gathered at the main gate. He was more astonished to see tears of grief and sadness openly flowing down the cheeks of many men. Spontaneously, the acting warden issued an unheard of order within the prison system. He gave the men permission to leave the prison and walk to the Lawes' home where they could pay their final respects. All day long, a parade of convicted felons walked three-quarters of a mile to stand in line and say goodbye to Catherine Lawes. In spite of the fact the men left the prison unaccompanied by guards, that night every single prisoner checked back into prison. Not one took advantage of the opportunity to escape.

The quality that transformed so many hardened lives in that prison was Catherine Lawes' gentle spirit. Her impact clearly demonstrates that gentleness is powerful, strong, vigorous, dynamic, and life changing. What our world desperately needs now is an outbreak of gentleness. Knowing that there would always be a shortage of gentleness may be what inspired the Apostle Paul to include this virtue in his fruit of the spirit list: "When the Holy Spirit controls our lives, he will produce this kind of fruit in us: love, joy, peace, patience, kindness, goodness, faithfulness, *gentleness* and self-control." (Gal 5:22-23). Here are some ways of infusing our society with gentleness.

• *Begin by cultivating gentle thoughts.* Gentleness starts in the mind. The actions of our lives are tinged by the color and complexion of our thoughts. We become what we think so be sure to entertain gentle thoughts, loving thoughts, kind thoughts, good thoughts, compassionate thoughts about yourself, about people. Begin by examining your mind and thoughts. Do you see the world as a hostile, uninviting, unaccepting place? Are you guilty of viewing others in a negative, critical, judgmental way? If so, tame your mind and train yourself to think differently. Consider this analogy: if you wish to build bigger biceps and increase muscle mass, you will need to practice weight lifting in a very disciplined way. Similarly, if you wish to live in a way that is gentle, inviting and embracing, you will need to practice overcoming every tendency to be pessimistic, cynical, and skeptical. Be guided by these words of Scripture: "Let your mind be filled with whatever is true, honorable and just. Think about things that are excellent and worthy of praise" (Phil 4:8).

• *Be gentle in spirit.* Interestingly, the linguistic origins of the word "gentle" refer to a wild animal that has been tamed. For example, a formerly wild horse which has been tamed and

harnessed is described as "gentled" or a "gentling." Any animal that has been "gentled" becomes useful: A horse can pull
a wagon; an ox can plow; an elephant can carry cargo. Thus,
to be gentle is to use our strength in a helpful and focused way.
Here is an example from professional ice hockey, regarded by
many as a rough sport made up of large, tough athletes. Yet,
even in that physical and sometimes violent arena there are
athletes with tender hearts and gentle spirits. When the Dallas
Stars won the coveted Stanley Cup in 1999, a first for their
team, they learned that each player was entitled to take the
cup home for a twenty-four hour period. Normally each player carries the Stanley Cup back to his hometown proudly plac-
ing it on display for his family and friends. Joe Nieuwendyk,
one of the Stars key players, begged and pleaded to have the
cup an extra day so he could take it to two sites. The first day
he took it to Whitby, Ontario where he grew up playing hockey. There he put the Stanley Cup in the local hockey arena
where many of the town's youth teams came by to view it and
be inspired by it.

However, Nieuwendyk had a special and personal reason
for asking authorities to let him have the cup an additional
day. The following morning he took the Stanley Cup to Ithaca,
NY where he had been a student at Cornell University. There,
his favorite professor was Dan Sisler, who is blind. "I had a lot
of respect for him," Nieuwendyk said. The hockey player held
a special reception at Cornell primarily for Sisler's benefit.
"Everyone stopped what they were doing to see him going
over the Cup. It was awesome. It was a neat feeling to see him
scan the Cup with his hands," Nieuwendyke recalls.

• *Be gentle with those who have hurt you.* As we go through life, various people will hurt us through their words and acts or through neglect. Rather than harbor angry or hateful thoughts in your mind and heart, respond to their wounding in a gentle way by extending forgiveness. Live by this wisdom from Martin Luther King, Jr.: "Forgiveness is not an occasional act, it is a permanent attitude."

• *Be gentle toward the less fortunate.* The Bible notes that people who exhibit divine wisdom are "peace loving, gentle at all times . . . full of mercy and good fruits" (Jas 3:17). Be especially gentle and merciful with those who are less fortunate and in deep pain and suffering. Former television evangelist Jim Bakker who was convicted and jailed says his life was saved through a gentle prison guard who responded to him with kindness and mercy. Early in his imprisonment Bakker experienced a nervous breakdown. "I felt isolated and rejected, as though no one knew what was happening to me, or nobody cared. The constant, horrendous din of the place (prison) was driving me over the edge," he writes in his book, *I Was Wrong.* "I finally got to the place where I could take no more. I decided to allow myself to go insane. I dropped to the floor in the corner of the cell, close to the door. It was the one spot in the room where no eyes could see me."

Just as Bakker was letting go of his will to live, he heard a voice call out: "Jim, God loves you!" Believing he was hallucinating, Bakker heard the same voice a second time saying: "Jim, God loves you!" He looked up and saw "two eyes filled with compassion looking at me through the slot in the door." The voice belonged to the prison guard who was on duty. In a quiet tone, he spoke other encouraging words to Bakker and prayed with him. "When he finished praying, I knew there was a God in prison, even though I could not sense His presence in my own life just then," Bakker writes. After the prayer, the guard asked Bakker not to tell anyone about their spiritual encounter because the guard feared he would be fired. "I shall never forget that servant of God who risked his livelihood to save my life, for whether he knew it or not, that is exactly what he did," Bakker writes.

• *Extend gentleness toward every person you encounter daily.* Make it your daily practice to treat, with gentleness, each member of your family, your neighbors, work colleagues, those who serve you through their jobs and even strangers you meet. "How far you go in life depends on your being tender with the young, compassionate with the aged, sympathetic with the striving, and tolerant of the weak and the strong— because someday you will have been all of these," said George Washington Carver. Recently a man wrote an advice columnist saying he and his wife were celebrating his 87th birthday at a fine restaurant in Hollywood, Florida. While ordering their meal, his hearing aid fell out and bounced off his chest. As the elderly man stood up to begin a search, his chair bumped a patron sitting directly behind. He apologized to the young man and explained why he stood up. The young man immediately got down on his hands and knees joining the 87-year-old in searching for the hearing aid under the table.

When their search produced no results, the young man suggested that the senior citizen look in his shirt pocket. Sure enough, that was where the hearing aid had landed. "I was elated, shook hands with the young man and his female companion and told them they had made our day," he said. Upon finishing their meal, the elderly couple asked for their check. "No check," the waitress replied. "The meal was paid for by the young man who helped you find your hearing aid." The elderly man went on to explain: "I have written this letter to you and your readers to prove that cynicism is not the order of the day. There are still good people everywhere." Such is the power of the gentle!

Seven Further Considerations

1. Conduct an examination of yourself asking: Are my thoughts gentle or harsh? Do I respond to others with gentleness or inconsiderately?

2. When someone offends or hurts you, how do you treat them? Could you find a more gentle way of responding?

3. Think about and describe a time when you experienced gentleness from someone.

4. What mindset is necessary for you to become a more gentle person?

5. Think back over the last few weeks and try to recall media stories about people who acted gently. Why did they make the news?

6. Why does it take strength, not weakness, to be gentle?

7. What is the meaning of this statement by Gandhi: "In a gentle way you can shake the world?"

HABIT #9 - SELF-CONTROL

The Fruit of the Spirit Is ... Self-Control

I am indeed a king because
I know how to rule myself.
—Pietro Aretino

SEVERAL years ago psychologist Walter Mischel conducted what has become a classic social experiment. He left a group of 4-year-olds in a room with a bell and a marshmallow. He told them if they rang the bell, he would come back and they could eat the marshmallow. If, however, they chose not to ring the bell and wait for him to return on his own, they would then be given two marshmallows. In videos of the experiment, the children could be seen squirming, kicking, hiding their eyes desperately trying to exercise self-control to wait it out in order to have two marshmallows. Some broke down and rang the bell within a minute. Others lasted 15 minutes. Tracking those children for several years Mischel made these discoveries: the ones who waited longer went on to get higher SAT scores; they got into better colleges and had, on average, better adult outcomes. On the other hand, the children who rang the bell quickest were more likely to become bullies. They received worse teacher and parental evaluations ten years later and were more likely to have drug problems by age 32.

Mischel's experiment is worth noting because it demonstrates clearly that self-control is essential for successful, satisfying living. Low self-control appears to be part of low self-esteem. People who are self-controlled can delay gratification and sit through difficult or boring classes in order to graduate. People who are self-disciplined can perform rote, monotonous tasks—such as those required to master a language. With self-control women and men can avoid drugs, alcohol, and other self-defeating habits. For people lacking in the life skill of self-control life becomes a parade of foolish decisions: truancy, school failure, teen pregnancy, obesity, drug, alcohol, and gambling addiction. That's why self-control has been encouraged by sages across the centuries. Benjamin Franklin advised: "If passion drives you, let reason hold the reins." British poet Alfred Lord Tennyson wrote: "The happiness of a man in this life does not consist in the absence but in the mastery of his passions." The book of Proverbs notes: "Like a city with no defenses is a man who lacks self-control" (Prov 25:28). This virtue ends St. Paul's list of spiritual fruit: "The fruit of the spirit is . . . *self-control*" (Gal 5:23). Though this quality has been highly endorsed by sages and Scripture writers, it's a sad reality that too many people are running out of self-control. Here are some methods and moments for tapping into the power of self-control.

• *Make self-control a life priority.* You may not succeed with every effort at self-control but if you make it a top life priority the odds of success are much more in your favor. Remind yourself of this basic biblical teaching about self-control: "Better a patient man than a warrior, a man who controls his temper than one who takes a city" (Prov 16:32).

John Jay (1743-1829), the first chief justice of the U.S. Supreme Court, made self-control a key virtue of his life. After losing the 1792 gubernatorial race in New York (later he would serve two terms as governor), he wrote to his wife. Rather than lament his loss, he reminded himself and his wife about the priority of self-control: "A few more years will put us all in the dust, and it will then be of more importance to me to have governed myself than to have governed the state."

- *Take a disciplined approach to a life crisis.* Rather than respond with panic when life presents an unexpected and traumatic challenge say to yourself, "I have self-control and I will use it in this situation." Doing so will cut down on a natural tendency to come apart and enable you to offer a more healthy, creative approach. When David Fajgenbaum was 18-years-old, he received the horrible news his mother was diagnosed with brain cancer. He was just preparing for a new life as a freshman at Georgetown University. Instead of plunging into the typical college life, David spent every weekend at home with family. "I had three feelings: I felt alone, I felt helpless, and I felt guilty for being at school," he recalls. Instead of continuing to live with uncertainty and fear, David decided to honor his mother by creating meaning out of her terminal illness. He began to reach out to others who were going through the same thing at school. Returning to the campus, he learned that beyond ordinary counseling, the university had no services for grieving students. So David launched a support group: *Students of Ailing Mothers and Fathers.* His project evolved rapidly and the organization now has more than 20 chapters including some among younger teens who are still in high school. Even after his mother died, David did not withdraw but continued guiding the organization three or four hours daily. "I invested everything in it. It's the most reward-ing thing, to honor somebody and at the same time to be able to have an impact."

• *Learn from others.* Be the most coachable person on the planet. Look around and identify people who are role models of self-control and self-discipline. Study their behavior careful-ly and then incorporate it into your own life. Also, ask them for guidance. Apply to your life this teaching of Jesus: "Ask, and it will be given to you; seek, and you will find; knock, and the door will be opened to you. For everyone who asks will receive; those who seek will find; and to those who knock, the door will be opened" (Mt 7:7-8). One who practices this is Harvey Mackay. He is a best-selling author, syndicated colum-nist, CEO of a major corporation, a speaker in great demand, a prominent civic leader, a marathoner, and one of the top ama-teur tennis players in his home state of Minnesota. One of his "secrets" to success: he actively seeks out and allows himself to learn from others. "You don't have to know everything, as long as you know people who know the things you don't," he says. "There's a lot that I don't know, so I shamelessly ask for advice."

• *Practice self-regulation.* This means developing the abili-ty to handle and manage your emotions especially when facing disappointment and distress. Staying calm, thinking clearly, seeing objectively under such stress is essential for per-sonal effectiveness. One who does this is Emeril Lagasse. Today he is a celebrity television chef. However, his start on television was weak and his programs were cancelled twice. The first show, *How To Boil Water*, was launched but didn't connect with viewers. Lagasse and the Food Network cable channel decided to try again. The next season they launched his second show, *Emeril and Friends*. This failed as well. Producers and viewers said Emeril appeared stiff and uncomfortable on camera. Emeril practiced emotional self-regulation, refused to panic and quit, persuading the network to give him one final opportunity. This time, he took charge of the entire show picking his own recipes, using his own words and taping before a live audience. The result: his enthusiastic spirit and ability to connect with a live group created one of the most popular cooking shows on television.

• *Tell yourself: practice perfects.* As you practice the fine art of self-control you will become better at it. Over time you will strengthen your mental and emotional approach to life. Rather than react with panic you will respond in a more rational, reasoned style. The story is told of a clever jester who was employed by the royal court. For years he always amused the royal family and their aides. One day, in a careless moment, he managed to offend the King who ordered him put to death. "However, in consideration of your many years of fine and faithful service," the king said, "I'll let you choose how you wish to die." Pausing only briefly to collect his thoughts, the jester responded: "Oh, mighty king, I thank you for this great kindness. I choose death . . . by old age."

• *Challenge your excuses.* When life gets hard, when the challenge feels overwhelming, when it looks impossible—those are the times it's easy to come up with reasons why you can't triumph and overcome. Remind yourself they're just excuses which will keep you from getting to the next level.

Challenge your thinking. Eula Weaver is a woman who challenged all excuses not to practice self-discipline and self-control. At age seventy-seven, Eula was paralyzed with a stroke. It would have been easy for her to make excuses saying "I can't recover from this. At my age, this is it for me. I'm done!" Instead, she challenged every objection which came into her mind and tapped into a spirit of self-control. Because of the paralyzing stroke, the doctors told her she had two choices: 1) spend her remaining time as a bed-bound invalid or 2) get out of bed and begin walking no matter how painful and difficult. Slowly she forced herself out of bed and began taking a few steps. Some time later, the local newspaper featured Eula in a jogging suit running a mile per day at age eighty-eight.

In his book, *The 21 Indispensable Qualities of a Leader,* John C. Maxwell advises: "Get rid of excuses. Write down every reason why you might not be able to follow through with your disciplines. Read through them. You need to dismiss them as the excuses they are. Even if a reason seems legitimate, find a solution to overcome it. Don't leave yourself any reasons to quit. Remember, only in the moment of discipline do you have the power to achieve your dreams."

Seven Further Considerations

1. Think back to a time when you "lost it" and didn't show self-control. What was the result? How could you do things differently in the future?

2. Would you say that you generally take a disciplined or undisciplined approach to personal challenges?

3. Reflect on this statement by Oswald Chambers: "Beware of saying, 'I haven't time to read the Bible, or to pray'; say rather, 'I haven't disciplined myself to do these things.' "

4. Identify persons who are role models of self-control and self-discipline. Describe their qualities. How can you incorporate them into your living?

5. Has someone tried to help you exercise self-control? How did you respond, positively or negatively?

6. What excuses do you use to avoid dealing with life's harsh times? How can you offset those, exercise self-discipline, and deal effectively with difficulty?

7. What is the wisdom in this contemporary proverb: "You can't control what happens to you but you can control your attitude to what happens"?

Additional Titles Published by Resurrection Press, a Catholic Book Publishing Imprint

For a free catalog call 1-800-892-6657
www.catholicbookpublishing.com